One Day in the
ALPINE TUNDRA

Trophy Chapter Books by
Jean Craighead George:

ONE DAY IN THE TROPICAL RAIN FOREST
ONE DAY IN THE WOODS

And coming soon:

ONE DAY IN THE DESERT
ONE DAY IN THE PRAIRIE

One Day in the ALPINE TUNDRA

by Jean Craighead George
illustrated by Walter Gaffney-Kessell

HarperTrophy®
A Division of HarperCollinsPublishers

Harper Trophy® is a registered trademark of HarperCollins Publishers Inc.

Library of Congress Cataloging-in-Publication Data
George, Jean Craighead, date
  One day in the alpine tundra / by Jean Craighead George ; illustrated
by Walter Gaffney-Kessell
    p.   cm.
  Summary: Relates a boy's adventure when he is alone on the alpine
tundra on a stormy day.
    ISBN 0-690-04325-2. — ISBN 0-690-04326-0 (lib. bdg.)
    ISBN 0-06-442027-2 (pbk.)
    1. Mountain ecology—Wyoming—Rendezvous Mountain—
Juvenile literature.   2. Tundra ecology—Wyoming—Rendezvous
Mountain—Juvenile literature.   3. Rendezvous Mountain (Wyo.)—
Juvenile literature.   [1. Mountain ecology.   2. Tundra ecology.
3. Rendezvous Mountain (Wyo.)   4. Landslides.   5. Ecology]
I. Gaffney-Kessell, Walter, ill.   II. Title.
QH105.W8G46   1984   82-45590
574.5'2644'0978755   CIP
                                                                      AC

❖

First Harper Trophy edition, 1996.

One Day in the
ALPINE TUNDRA

Chapter 1

An hour after sunrise on August 16th, a huge slab of rock slipped. It lay at 10,000 feet on the top of Rendezvous Mountain in the Teton Mountains of Wyoming. It had been cracking in the heat and cold for centuries, and now on August 16th at 7:20 A.M. was poised to fall.

A snowfall, a wind blast of more than 30 miles per hour, even the vibrations from a thunderclap, would be all that was needed to send the monolith crashing five hundred feet onto the alpine tundra.

Below, on the fall line of the slab of rock, Johnny Moore was sleeping in his mountain tent in the grass of a meadow.

The wind blew softly. A mountaintop is a land of great peace or great violence.

At 8 A.M. a marmot, the woodchuck of the high country, left his burrow in a boulder field and climbed to his lookout post.

Perched under the teetering chunk of rock, he whistled a shrill note reminiscent of a boy calling his dog. The whistle told other marmots who he was—the boss of

this boulder field. Having made his
statement, he sneezed, then sat up on his
haunches. Under him was a mat of
orange lichens.

Lichens are the pioneer plants of
the mountaintops, growing at higher

altitudes than all others. Half algae, half fungus, the flat gray-green, orange, black, purple and red plants need only a nick in a rock to get a roothold, and a spray of snowmelt or rain to grow on.

The rock hung quietly above the alpine tundra.

The alpine tundra is a community of plants and animals that have adapted to the harsh climate on the tops of tall mountains. It begins where the trees stop growing. It is a land of grass, wild-flowers, mosses and animals that can find food and shelter among these plants.

The alpine tundra is made up of

4

several smaller communities. The big boulders break into rocks, the rocks into stones, the stones into gravel and scree. The scree breaks up into sand. As they roll, the pieces sort themselves by size. The big boulders are at the lowest level; the others are higher. Each has its own plants and animals. Marmots and lichens live in the boulder fields. The

little pika, a close relative of the rabbits, lives with the dandelions on the rocky talus slopes. Meadow mice (voles), weasels, mosses and grass live on the fell-fields, or stone fields. There are snow beds, or marshes where the snow-fields have melted. Here sedges grow and insects dwell. Even the unmelted snowfield is a home: Algae and primitive insects, the springtails, live on the icy surface.

At the down-mountain edge of the alpine tundra lies the krummholz, clusters of dwarfed trees that have been twisted by the wind and crushed by the ice. Birds and an occasional bull elk find shelter here. Up-mountain from the krummholz the wind is so strong, the soil so cold, the growing season so short, that no trees can grow. This wild, fresh wilderness is called the alpine tundra, the land above the trees.

It is beset by bad weather: blizzards, high winds, unremitting ice, lightning

6

and blazing sunlight. At 10,000 feet there is 25 percent more light than at sea level, and twice as much ultraviolet radiation. Water is scarce on the tundra. In winter it is not available because it is frozen. In spring and summer the snowmelt and rain run off through the rocks and sand, leaving the soils dry.

Geological disasters beset the alpine tundra. Snows avalanche, glaciers scour and cut. The wind, water and ice erode; and monoliths split off, fall and crash down on the wild things.

The alpine tundra in the United States lies atop the tallest mountains, under the clouds or in radiant sun. It is on the summits of the Sierra Nevada and Southern Cascade Mountains in California; on the Olympic Mountains and Northern Cascades of Washington; on the tops of the Rockies in Idaho, Montana, Wyoming and Colorado; on the peaks of the Great Basin Ranges in Nevada, Utah, Oregon and California.

In the east, the alpine tundra is found

on the summits of the Presidential Range of the White Mountains of New Hampshire, the Adirondacks of New York and Mount Katahdin in Maine.

The farther north the mountains lie, the lower the alpine tundra begins. In Southern California's Sierra Nevada it starts at 10,500 feet. In the Teton Mountains of Wyoming it appears at approximately 9,500 feet, and in the Cascades and Olympic Mountains at 6,500 feet. The alpine tundra on the Presidential Range of New Hampshire is low, between 4,200 and 5,000 feet, because a major east-west storm path passes over these mountains. Winds of over 300 miles per hour have been recorded on Mount Washington. This kills trees and most plants.

Chapter 2

At 8:20 A.M. Johnny rolled over in his sleeping bag and hit the side of his tent.

The marmot saw the tent move and whistled a warning to the alpine community. Frightened, he dove into a crack between the boulders.

The rock hung quietly.

Johnny and his father had climbed to the alpine meadow the day before. Johnny enjoyed the sharp, clear air and the special glisten of the alpine tundra.

He had spent the night alone, promising to join his father, a forest ranger, at sundown this day.

At 8:35 A.M. he was still asleep. The low oxygen content of the alpine air is tiring until the lungs and body adjust. He turned onto his stomach.

At 8:40 A.M. a flock of water pipits, buffy-brown sparrow-sized birds of the alpine tundra, winged out of the grass on the fell-field and flew to the top of the snowfield. With a constant bobbing of their tails, they caught the tiny spring-tails that were gathered on the snow in dark clusters. The creatures hop around by releasing a sticklike appendage on their stomachs. It strikes the ground with a snap and catapults the springtail up and down to another spot, making it look like a kid on a pogo stick.

Where the pipits stepped, red foot-prints appeared. Their weight had squashed the rose-red coats of the snow algae. The color is anthocyanin, a red pigment alpine plants manufacture to

10

survive. It collects heat and warms them so they can grow even in the snow. The water pipits flew to the edge of an alpine pond.

By 9 A.M. the gentle wind of early morning had become a whistler. It blew shrill tunes on the grass blades and made lugubrious notes as it passed over the cracks between the rocks in the boulder field. It shook Johnny's tent

pole, but only nudged the chickweed plants growing low on the ground by his door. The higher the wind is above the ground, the stronger it blows. The alpine plants have adjusted to this. They do not grow more than a few inches tall, keeping out of the scissor clip of the wind. They have also adapted to the high radiation. Many put out red leaves. Anthocyanin also absorbs the ultraviolet rays and fends off death by radiation.

Only a few plants and animals live

on the alpine tundra, because of the wind and ice and radiation. Fewer than 200 kinds of plants survive there, as compared to more than 100 million kinds in the tropics. Only 7 species of mammals live on the alpine tundra. The tropics support more than 500 species. No amphibians, reptiles or fish can live in the tundra's streams and ponds; and only one bird, the ptarmigan, with its feathered feet and toes, stays all year round on the alpine tundra.

Chapter 3

The tent was motionless. Johnny slept. The marmot whistled "All's well" and waddled down from his lookout boulder. Where he had sat, an orange lichen grew. It thrived on the urine left by the marmot. Other orange mats on the boulders, marking other lookout spots, polka-dotted the rocks.

Crossing the snowfield, the marmot frightened the water pipits. In the snow bed left by the melting snowfield he ate a few tender shoots, then plodded on. He arrived in the fell-field, a community of medium-sized stones, sand, soil and ingenious plants like the alpine dandelion, which had gone to seed. The round puffs were breaking up in the wind and sailing off to alight and put down roots.

The dandelion is well suited for life in the rugged fell-field. Its leaves grow in a rosette flat against the ground and out of the wind. Its thick root holds it in place when the stones shift. The root, which is abnormally long, searches out the water under the dry fell-field.

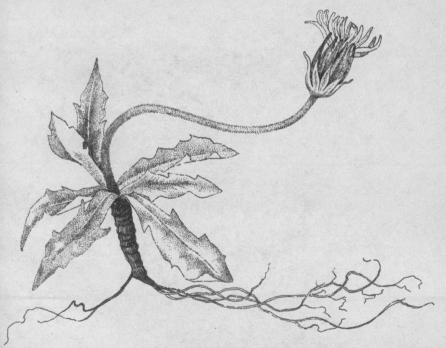

All summer the marmot had been putting on weight in preparation for his winter hibernation. On August 16th he was sleek and fat, but he moved quickly despite his weight, for like all animals of the alpine tundra he has a heart that beats faster than those of his cousins in the valleys as it pumps the scant oxygen through his bloodstream. On this day he, like the other creatures of the alpine tundra, was in a race against time.

Spring, summer and fall are compacted into less than three months at 10,000 feet, and it was already autumn. The asters were blooming, the tufted hair grass had turned golden, the mountain blue violet leaves had withered and fallen.

The marmot was in the first stage of hibernation. He was sleepy. His head drooped and nodded as he ate. A heavy frost two nights ago had set off his internal sleep clock. He was slowing down toward the hour when he would waddle into his den, put his paws over his nose, tuck his head in his groin and hibernate. His body temperature would drop to almost 34° F., his heart rate would slow down and he would breathe only once or twice a day. In winter torpor he would live through the foodless subzero temperatures under the ice and snow.

At 9:20 A.M. a mother pika came out of her den in the talus slope. Unlike the lowland rabbits, this creature of the mountaintops has small ears that are

17

close to her head to protect them from frostbite. The pads of her feet are covered with fur, not only for warmth but to hold her to icy rocks, for she is up all winter running through her labyrinth of tunnels that wind between and around the stones of the talus slope.

She can stay up all winter because she is a food storer. During the summer she harvests the wildflowers and grasses of the alpine tundra and places them on rocks in the sun. When they are dry, she stores them in her hay bins among the

tumbled rocks, and feeds on them through blizzard and cold while the marmot sleeps.

By August 16th the pika had mated and raised one litter of four youngsters, who were now harvesting their own crops for the winter.

The smallest of her offspring was in the snowbed. With a snip of his four cutting teeth he felled a three-inch sedge. Another of her youngsters was running across the alpine meadow with

a red flower of the gilia in her mouth. She placed it beside a pile of blue gentians and white bitterroot to make a red-white-and-blue haypile. She piped a soft note, turned and went back to work.

Chapter 4

At 9:35 A.M. Johnny thrust his head out of his tent door and looked out over the drop-off of the glacial bowl or amphitheater where the alpine tundra was nestled. A raven, his wings spread motionlessly, was riding a spiraling wind up and out of the subalpine forest, the community of plants and animals below the alpine tundra. He circled over the meadow watching for meadow mice, fledgling birds and small pikas; saw none and sped to the teetering rock. He alighted there.

It held.

21

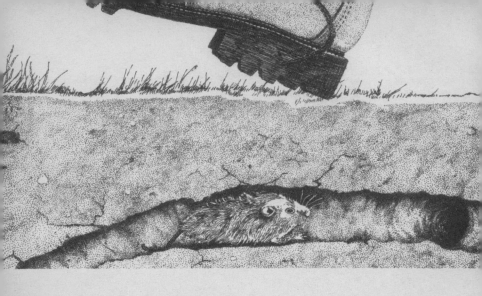

Johnny dressed, rolled up his sleeping bag and sat down to pull on his mountain boots. He kicked the ground as he rammed his foot into place.

A pocket gopher in his tunnel under the tent felt the earth quake. He stopped and listened. He was about the size of a red squirrel, sported an almost furless tail and had small golden ears. The gopher's fur was dusty with soil. He had been on his way underground to the fell-field when the earth had shaken. He was nervous this morning and irritable. A meadow mouse had dug into one of his storage bins and stolen his seeds and roots. Furthermore, a weasel had entered one of his tunnel entrances, and weasels eat gophers.

Johnny put on his other boot and kicked the ground. The gopher plowed like a Roto-Rooter into another of his tunnels and ran to his bedroom. He curled up in his nest of dry grass.

The pocket gopher is the farmer of the alpine tundra. He plows up the deep soil. He buries seeds in his storage bins, thereby protecting them from the deep freeze of winter so that they survive to grow in spring. He aerates the soil with several hundred feet of tunnels, and adds minerals to it with his excreta. When he tunnels to the surface, he kicks up a mound of dirt called a gopher esker. On these mounds grow special plants that can live only on disturbed soil.

At 9:45 A.M. the pocket gopher peered out of his bedroom door and listened. The earth did not shake again. He ran down a shaft that led under the alpine

23

marsh. With a vigorous kick of his hind feet he threw up the earth and emerged in a shower of soil. He sniffed and listened. Water chimes were sounding. The underside of the snowfield had begun to melt in the morning sun. The drips pooled, spilled over and sparkled down the streambed. They poured into the alpine pond at the edge of the krummholz.

The pocket gopher stuffed his cheek pouches with sedge seeds, dove into his hole and carried them back to his pantry. He emptied his cheeks by pushing his

paws over his fur-lined pouches. He then turned them inside out and cleaned them. Special muscles snapped them back into place.

The pantry was too small for any more seeds. The gopher studied the problem and solved it by digging to enlarge it. He broke into the nest of a water shrew, a member of the shrew family, the smallest North American mammals. The shrew curled back the lips on his pointed snout and hissed at the gopher, showing all thirty of his black-tipped teeth. His tiny eyes, which can see only light and dark, twinkled. The gopher backed away, for water shrews can bite hard. He sealed the hole and enlarged the pantry in another direction.

Irritated by the delays of the morning, the gopher finished this job with a spray of dirt and went back to his underground farm beneath the alpine marsh. He tore bark off the runners of a sedge. To survive the short growing season that is sometimes too brief for the sedge

seeds to set, these plants send out underground runners, or rhizomes, that
sprout new plants.

The water shrew was now wide
awake. He leaped out of his den, sped
like an arrow to the alpine pond and dove
in. Encased in a coat of air bubbles, he
swam gracefully to the bottom, where he
stood on his head and caught mayfly
larvae. After eating voraciously, he sur-
faced and came ashore. He was not even
wet.

A weasel lying in the doorway of his
den saw the shrew on the pond shore
and tightened his muscles to spring.

But the shrew had smelled the

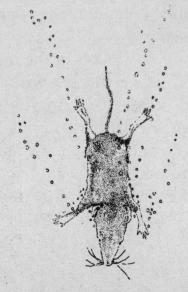

weasel. With an explosion of energy, he crossed the pond on top of the water, supported by his swift motion and, in part, by water tension. Dashing ashore, he wove into the cracks between the rocks in the fell-field. The weasel came to the pond edge, reared to his hind legs and looked for the shrew. A bobbing red flower caught his attention. At its base a vole, or meadow mouse, was eating.

The weasel stole toward him, frightening the water pipits feeding in the marsh. They burst like rockets around him, white tail feathers flashing the "Follow me" signal of these birds. They alighted beside a flock of white-throated sparrows, who were hunting seeds. The sparrows were restless. Autumn had come to their tundra home. The shortening hours of daylight were changing the hormones in their bodies. They were feeling an urge to migrate down the mountain to the gardens and town lawns in the Wyoming lowlands.

The weasel, meadow mouse held

27

firmly in his teeth, charged the sparrows playfully. They flew up before him, circled the snow bed and, with chips and cries, suddenly flew over the krummholz and down the mountain. At 10 A.M. on August 16th their migration had begun.

Chapter 5

At 10:30 A.M. the wind changed from whistling gusts to a steady blow. The sun had warmed the land at the foot of the mountain. The heated air was rising, forming an upslope wind. With each 1,000 feet it climbed, the warm wind lost three degrees of heat. The hotter the valley, the faster the wind blew, until it was strong enough to carry sand and dust. Like an abrasive air gun it came over the krummholz and sandblasted the boulder field and the wall of the amphitheater. It pitted the huge rock.

The great slab held.

At 11 A.M. the sand-bearing wind clipped the top off a dwarf willow growing near Johnny's tent. And it stung the nose of a bull elk resting beside the krummholz. He got to his feet and snorted.

The bull elk fed all year round on the alpine tundra, grazing the grasses when the winter winds blew the snow from them. By day and the dark of night he bedded down in the shelter of the krummholz. All the morning of the 16th of August, he had felt the first restlessness of the mating season. With a click of his hooves he ran a few steps and, lifting his head, bugled a halfhearted courtship call to his harem.

In late September he would join these cows in the subalpine forest. He would fight off any bull elk who dared to come near. After the mating season he would return to the tundra.

The elk turned his back on the sandy wind, leaped over a clump of krummholz and trotted a few yards down the footpath Johnny had climbed. He paused and sniffed the wind. It smelled of storm.

The monolith of rock hung on the cliff top.

The elk paused to graze grass before the storm set in.

At 12:20 P.M. the marmot whistled "danger." A goshawk was overhead. Like the raven, he had ridden a spiraling wind out of the subalpine forest. His red eyes gleamed as he studied the meadow.

The water pipits saw him and darted under the leaves of a scarlet paintbrush and the seeding lupine.

The marmot ran under a rock, where he could watch the large hawk without being seen. The weasel hid under a crust of the dripping snowfield.

The pocket gopher was still working underground, safe from the eyes of the hawk.

The smallest pika was running toward his hay rock with a red flower. It flut-

tered like a bright flag. The goshawk dove.

At 12:45 P.M. the wind was gusting at 22 miles per hour across the alpine meadow.

Johnny avoided the wind chill by eating his peanut-butter sandwich on

the lee side of the krummholz. The valleys and mountains beyond were misty with dust blown up from the dry valleys.

The goshawk arose from the grass at the foot of the talus slope. He beat his wings as he flew over Johnny, then he plunged into the subalpine forest.

Chapter 6

At 1:30 P.M. little cloud puffs formed in the sky. When the wind blew stronger, Johnny lay down on his back to get out of the blow. He picked his spot carefully so as not to lie on the forget-me-nots, gentians and seeding bistorts. Footsteps, tents and people, his father had said, could crush the alpine plants, and it would take ten or twenty years for them to recover.

The white clouds came together, piled up and darkened.

On the wind from the subalpine

 34

forest rode a magnificent golden eagle. He soared up and over the krummholz. The hackles on his head flapped like ribbons in the wind. Slowly he turned his head from the right to the left as he watched the ground for prey. From half a mile up he saw the trembling whisker of the pocket gopher in his hole in his dirt mound. He slowed his flight.

The marmot, who could see both down and up at the same time, observed the eagle and whistled "danger."

The water pipits heard and sat still.

In her small bedroom under the talus slope the mother pika did not hear the cry of the marmot. She came to her den entrance, but did not see the eagle. She did, however, smell the storm. To be stopped in her food gathering for the duration of a thunderstorm could mean a day without food in the spring. Very often the alpine plants do not start to grow until mid-June because of bad weather, and pikas with short supplies could starve in their burrows.

She dashed to the alpine meadow and cut down a buckwheat stem with seeds. As she carried it to her drying rock, she passed the haystack of her smallest offspring. He had not been back to his pile since the goshawk had come and gone. She called him with a soft piping sound. He did not answer. She picked up his dry flowers and pushed them under a rock out of the storm.

The plants of the haystack were an odd-looking harvest. They were quite different from the same plants in the valley, for alpine plants do not waste energy producing big leaves and long stems. Their stems are short, their leaves nubby and few. Almost all their energy goes into making flowers and seeds.

At 2:45 P.M. the wind reached 27 miles per hour, evaporating water from the stems and leaves of the alpine plants.

A saxifrage plant drew on the water stored in its thick leaves.

The wind blew. The rock held still.

Chapter 7

Swiftly now, the cumulus clouds piled into thunderheads, the thunderheads into anvils and castles. They covered the sun. Instantly the temperature dropped, for the thin alpine air does not hold heat.

The mother pika picked up a dry, blue sky pilot flower and carried it through a hidden side entrance to her den. Squeezing under a stone, she let herself down a steep shaft into a pantry. She put the flower down and turned to go back to work.

The weasel was stretched out in his doorway watching the golden eagle. A buckwheat plant bobbed beside him. He bit it to keep it from catching the eye of the eagle. The eagle saw the weasel.

Rolling and churning, the storm clouds came down on Rendezvous Peak. Thunder boomed. The bull elk heard and stopped eating. The storm, he sensed, was a miserable thing, full of rain, hail and snow—graupel. He took the trail to the sub-alpine forest.

At 3:20 P.M. the wind stopped blowing. A stillness descended upon the alpine tundra. Not even a grass blade twisted, no birds flew or sang. The pond gleamed like polished steel.

Johnny got to his feet. He did not like to be caught on the mountain in a storm. He decided to meet his father early.

He packed his tent and sleeping bag in his backpack, shouldered it and glanced around. Suddenly he wanted to stay here. His head was light. He felt wonderful. The high altitude had given

39

him a false sense of well-being. He climbed upward, wishing to stay on the alpine tundra forever.

A bolt of lightning shot out of the clouds and lit up the rocks of Rendezvous Peak.

"One, two," Johnny counted. *Ka-boom.* Thunder shook the peak and rattled the boulders.

The huge rock held.

"Close," Johnny said aloud. "I've got to get out of here." But he did not. He climbed higher.

At the bottom of the boulder field he was struck in the face by a white blast of hail and rain.

"Graupel," he cried, coming to his senses. "I'll freeze to death." He forced

himself to turn around. Now he could
see nothing but white snow and hail. He
dropped to all fours to feel his way
down the trail.

A lightning bolt sizzled out of the
graupel. Johnny remembered that lightning travels down wet streambeds. He
was in a wet streambed. Another bolt

41

shot out of the clouds. The rocks around him buzzed.

Struggling to his feet, skidding and sliding on the round, icy hailstones, he ran. Suddenly the graupel stopped falling.

The wind struck the monolith of rock at 30 miles per hour.

It hung free in space.

Then it fell.

Chapter 8

The rock struck the wall of the amphitheater and exploded into a thousand cannonading boulders. The boulders bounced, blew up and were splintered into a million stones. The stones hit and shattered into gravel and scree, the scree into dust and sand. Then the mountainside avalanched. Rocks flowed like water.

Johnny could not hear the noise, but he felt it as a sharp pain in his ears. He screamed to relieve the pressure, and skidded into the alpine forest. Safe

43

among the trees, he glanced back.

A cloud of fine rock billowed up from the bottom of the amphitheater and obscured Rendezvous Peak. Now he heard the roar of devastation.

Johnny stared, then turned and ran full out down the mountain trail.

At 5 P.M. the debris had settled. The land was changed. The snowfield and snow bed were a boulder field, the fell-

44

field and scree were sand. The up-mountain side of the alpine meadow was a rock pile.

Only the talus slope was the same, for it had escaped the avalanche.

At 6:30 P.M. the air on the peak became cold and heavy. It flowed down the slope, carrying the stone dust with it.

At 7 P.M. the mother pika ran to her lookout rock. She piped, for she was confused by the land changes. The cold

wind struck her, and she ran to what was left of the alpine meadow to cut more plants. Winter was but weeks away.

She worked a few minutes, then sat up and looked at her world. The flash of the weasel was missing from the meadow, the marmot had not whistled. All the birds were gone.

At 7:30 P.M. the pocket gopher thrust his head out of his esker and, half blinded by the light, crept out onto the meadow. The wildflowers were gray with dust, a new boulder field was piled to his right, a new talus slope to his left. The stones that freckled the meadow were raw and new. No lichens grew on them.

He cried a thin peep, the only sound he could make, for gophers are quiet animals. He sniffed the air, then went back underground.

The sun set at 7:59 P.M., as it had every August 16th since the Earth was born. Rendezvous Peak was swathed in the pink of alpine glow.

In this mysterious light a breeze

dropped a fragment of lichen on the scar left by the fallen slab of rock. It sent out a root in the melt of a hailstone. The healing began.

Bibliography

Bare, Colleen Stanley. *Ground Squirrels*. New York: Dodd Mead. 1980.

George, Jean Craighead. *The Moon of the Mountain Lions*. New York: Thomas Y. Crowell, 1968.

Hester, Eugene et al. *Mountain Animals*. Chicago: Encyclopedia Britannica, 1979.

Jenkins, Marie M. *Deer, Moose, Elk and Their Family*. New York: Holiday House, 1979.

Johnson, Sylvia A. *Animals of the Mountains*. Minneapolis: Lerner Publications, 1980.

Nentl, Jerolyn Ann. *Mountain Climbing*. Nankato, Minn: Crestwood House, 1980.

Nicolson, Nigel. *The Himalayas, The World's Wild Places*. Amsterdam: Time-Life Books, 1975.

Index

Numbers in *italics* refer to illustrations

Don't miss this *One Day* chapter book:

One Day in the TROPICAL RAIN FOREST

by Jean Craighead George
illustrated by Gary Allen

It is dawn, and young Tepui makes his way through the rain forest. He treasures his homeland and all of its wildlife, from the giant trees to the playful monkeys to the colorful treetop birds.

But today is doomsday for Tepui's rain forest. Eleven bulldozers and four trucks will soon arrive to level the forest. Tepui is desperate to stop them, and there's just one way to do it. He must discover a butterfly no one has ever seen—by the end of the day.

Published by Harper Trophy Paperback Books

Don't miss this *One Day* chapter book:

One Day in the WOODS

by Jean Craighead George
illustrated by Gary Allen

There's a wizard hiding in the Teatown Woods, and Rebecca is determined to find it. Her uncle has told her about the beautiful ovenbird, "wizard of the woods," and she thinks it must be magic.

But when Rebecca sets out into the forest, she never expects to find magic everywhere she looks. A squirrel flies through the air. A deer vanishes before her eyes. And the mysterious ovenbird holds the greatest surprise of all. . . .

Published by Harper Trophy Paperback Books